SILVABAMBA

DAN D'AMELIO

A Pacemaker® Book

Fearon/Janus/Quercus
Belmont, California

Simon & Schuster Education Group

The PACEMAKER BESTELLERS

Bestellers I

Diamonds in the Dirt
Night of the Kachina
The Verlaine Crossing
Silvabamba
The Money Game

Flight to Fear
The Time Trap
The Candy Man
Three Mile House
Dream of the Dead

Bestellers II

Black Beach
Crash Dive
Wind Over Stonehenge
Gypsy
Escape from Tomorrow

The Demeter Star
North to Oak Island
So Wild a Dream
Wet Fire
Tiger, Lion, Hawk

Bestellers III

Star Gold
Bad Moon
Jungle Jenny
Secret Spy
Little Big Top

The Animals
Counterfeit!
Night of Fire and Blood
Village of Vampires
I Died Here

Bestellers IV

Dares
Welcome to Skull Canyon
Blackbeard's Medal
Time's Reach
Trouble at Catskill Creek

The Cardiff Hill Mystery
Tomorrow's Child
Hong Kong Heat
Follow the Whales
A Changed Man

Series Director: Tom Belina

Designer: Richard Kharibian

Cover and illustrations: Norman Nicholson

ISBN 0 - 8224 - 5255 - 3
Library of Congress Card Number: 77–74837

Printed in the United States of America.

10 9 8 7 6
MA

CONTENTS

CHAPTER 1

INTO THE UNKNOWN

Frank Pellon looked out the open door of the plane. Below him were the mountains of Silvabamba.

Frank turned to Ed Duval. "What do you think?" said Frank.

"Jumping might be a problem today," said Ed. "The wind is strong."

Frank looked out at the mountains below. For a year, he and Ed had planned to explore that part of Peru called Silvabamba. It was one of the few places left in the world that was still not explored. They knew if they put off their jump, it would be too late. The winter rains would begin soon.

Frank looked at Ed. "I think we should go," said Frank.

"Right," said Ed. "It's now or never."

Frank turned to the pilot. "Bring it down to 300 feet," he said.

The plane turned and headed down toward a clearing. Frank and Ed pulled a large bag to the plane door. Their sleeping bags and food were in the bag.

"Everything here?" Ed asked. "Yes," Frank answered. "I think so." "Then let's drop it."

When they were over the clearing, Frank and Ed pushed the bag out. They watched it fall into the tall grass below.

Then the plane climbed to 2,000 feet for the first jump run.

Frank held on to the sides of the plane door. Far below him, the clearing was just a tiny green spot.

Frank smiled at Ed. "See you later," he said.

Frank pushed hard with both hands and was gone. He sailed out and down.

Above him, the sound of the plane soon died as Frank fell toward Silvabamba.

He pulled the parachute handle. Suddenly his body jarred up as the parachute opened. For a minute, earth and sky seemed to be rocking up and down. Slowly the rocking stopped.

Frank could feel the air slipping by him. He was coming down into a world where no one from the outside world had ever set foot. What would he and Ed find in that unknown world? Would they be able to make their way through Silvabamba? Would they live to tell others what they found?

But it was too late now to worry about such things. Frank looked down on the green jungle of Silvabamba. He smiled. He had looked forward to this day for a long time. But, still, his mouth was dry and his heart was beating fast.

He grabbed the parachute's control lines and headed for the clearing. He pulled hard.

The wind was blowing him away from the clearing. It was blowing him toward the tall jungle trees. If he landed in the trees, he might be killed. Landing in a tree could break his back or his neck just like that.

Frank pulled again at the lines. He was still moving toward the trees.

He pulled on the control lines with all his might. It was working. He was moving toward the clearing again. At last.

Frank could still feel his heart pounding. But not as fast or as hard now.

The parachute jump had frightened him more than he thought it would. More than he would want anyone to know.

Now he was right over the clearing. He could see the bag they had dropped. The high grass of the clearing came rushing up at him.

Frank hit the ground and rolled.

He got up. Then he took off the parachute lines. He spotted Ed coming down at the end of the clearing. Frank ran to him.

"You OK?" asked Frank.

"Sure thing," said Ed. He smiled. "Welcome to Silvabamba."

The plane was flying in a circle above them. Frank and Ed waved. The plane's wings flashed in the sun. They watched the plane until it was out of sight.

Now the two men were alone. Ahead of them was the unknown world of Silvabamba.

CHAPTER 2
THE CANYON

Frank and Ed put on their packs. Then they picked up their guns and set off.

They moved into the high grass. The field of grass was long and wide. Far off, to their left, were low hills. They heard the cry of birds in trees all around them.

Frank stopped and pointed. A tree branch shook up and down. The men held their guns and waited. The tree branch shook again. Suddenly a loud cry rang out.

The men moved slowly toward the tree and looked up. Something was swinging from branch to branch. Then it stopped and looked down at them.

It was a monkey.

Frank and Ed looked at each other and laughed. "I was sure it was some strange, wild animal," said Ed.

"I guess we were strange to him," said Frank.

They set out again. Ahead of them now, they could see the dark lines of the jungle.

Above them, a green and yellow jungle bird flew in a circle. Its frightened cries filled the air.

The wind moved across the field of grass, bending the high, yellow grass in waves.

Suddenly, Ed stopped.

Frank looked at him. "What is it?"

"I saw something move," Ed said.

"Where?"

"Over there, in the grass," said Ed.

"What was it?"

"I couldn't tell," Ed said.

"Maybe it was the wind moving the grass," said Frank.

"No, it wasn't the—"

An Indian suddenly stood up in the grass. He pointed his bow at them.

Ed brought up his gun.

"Wait!" Frank shouted.

"What for?"

"If we hurt him, we'll never get out of Silvabamba alive," Frank said. "Put your gun down." Frank looked at the Indian.

The Indian was tall and strong-looking. His eyes were as dark as night. Around his neck was a string of teeth.

"Ed," Frank said, "look at those teeth around his neck."

Ed looked. "Yes," he said. "I see. They are human teeth."

Frank smiled at the Indian. *"Amigos. Friends,"* Frank said.

The Indian kept his bow pointed at them. *"Amigos,"* Frank said again. He forced himself to smile.

The Indian spoke. His voice was low. Another Indian stood up out of the grass. Then another. And another.

The first Indian stepped forward. He took a close look at Frank, then Ed.

"Smile at him," said Frank.

"I'd feel better if they smiled at us," Ed said. "I don't like the way they are fingering their bows.

"They have never seen people like us before," said Frank.

"If only they knew we dropped from the sky," said Ed.

Suddenly the Indian who had been standing before them turned to the other Indians. He pointed to the teeth around his neck. Then he looked at Frank and Ed. Several Indians stepped forward. They eyed Frank and Ed, then looked at each other.

"I think we are in trouble," Frank said. "I think they want to kill us and hang our teeth around their necks."

"Let's get out of here," Ed said. "If they try anything, shoot over their heads. That may frighten them."

With their eyes on the Indians, the men stepped back. Frank heard a noise behind him.

"Look out!" he shouted. Now there were Indians behind them, too. Ed brought up his gun and fired into the air.

The Indians stopped. They had never seen or heard a gun before.

Suddenly one of the Indians pointed at Frank and Ed with his bow. He was very tall. Around his neck were three strings of human teeth. His voice grew loud. Then he stopped. He drew his bow on Frank and Ed and fired an arrow. It almost hit Ed in the arm.

Ed fired his gun again. The Indians fell back. But they were not so frightened of the gun this time.

Frank and Ed started to run.

They headed across the field of grass. Frank looked back. Another Indian drew his bow. Then another and another. The air was filled with arrows.

"Come on!" shouted Ed. "Run for it. They are trying to kill us!"

An arrow flew by their legs. Another just missed Frank's head. They ran across the field toward the jungle.

"Look out!" Frank shouted. They came to a sudden stop. They were standing before a deep canyon.

The sides of the canyon were walls of rock, running straight up and down. The canyon was not wide. But it was very deep. At the bottom of the canyon, they could see a river. But they were too high above it to hear the splashing of the water.

They heard shouts behind them. The Indians were running through the field after them.

"Over there!" Ed said. He pointed to a tree near the canyon. They raced to the tree and hid behind it.

"Are they still coming?"

"Yes," Ed said. He raised his gun and fired. The shot smashed one Indian's bow. The Indians dropped into the grass.

"We can't hold them off for long," said Frank.

Ed eyed the grass. "We can try," he said.

Frank raised his head. "I don't see them," he said.

"They are still there," Ed said.

". . . Ed."

"What?"

"Look—there's a vine hanging down from the tree."

"So?"

"Maybe we can get across the canyon with it," said Frank. He took hold of the vine, then looked at the canyon.

"What's the matter?" said Ed.

"I don't think the vine is long enough to get us across," Frank said.

"There is only one way to find out," said Ed. "I'll cover you."

Frank took the vine and stepped back from the tree. Then, holding the vine, he ran. His body swung out over the canyon.

He hit the ground on the other side and rolled.

"OK, Ed." Frank threw the vine across to Ed.

Ed grabbed the vine, then looked back at the Indians. They had stopped and were just watching.

Ed stepped back, ran, and swung across the canyon.

He hit the ground, then came to his feet.

Now the Indians moved forward. One of them waved his arm at Frank and Ed and shouted some words at them.

"I think he is trying to tell us to come back across," said Frank.

"He must be kidding," said Ed.

Other Indians began waving and calling to Frank and Ed. Their voices seemed worried and afraid.

"What do you make of that?" Ed asked.

"I don't know," Frank answered. "It may be a trick. Let's keep moving before they decide to come after us."

Ahead of them was the jungle. It looked like a dark, green wall. The trees grew close together. Their thick branches seemed to be growing into each other.

Frank and Ed headed into the jungle. The Indians stood by the canyon, watching them.

Frank looked back. "That's strange," he said.

"What's strange?" Ed asked.

"The Indians are not following us," Frank said. "I wonder why."

Ed looked back. "Maybe they are afraid of our guns."

"Maybe so," said Ed.

It was getting dark. The sun was low over the trees.

"Let's find a spot to make camp," Frank said. "I think we are safe now."

They soon found a small clearing. Frank set up their tent. Ed started a fire.

When they finished eating, it was dark. The night air was cold. Frank and Ed threw more wood on the fire. Then they went into their tent. They placed their guns by their sides.

Frank turned. "Did you hear something?" he asked.

Ed shook his head.

Frank sat up. "Listen! Did you hear that?"

Ed listened. "It's nothing," he said. "Just the wind in the trees."

The men lay back in the dark night. Suddenly, there was a strange sound. Both men sat up.

"Glick-glick-glick."

"What was that?" Frank said.

Ed didn't answer. He looked out the tent. He spotted two eyes watching him.

"Glick-glick-glick."

Ed reached out of the tent. He picked up a stick and threw it.

Something ran into the dark jungle. Then it was still.

"What was it?" Frank asked.

"I don't know," said Ed. "Some kind of animal, I think."

The two men lay back, looking up into the black jungle. Then, listening to the night sounds, they slowly fell asleep.

CHAPTER 3

NO GOING BACK

Loud cries woke them up. Frank and Ed came out of the tent, their guns ready. It was early morning. The cries came from above, in the trees.

Suddenly a giant shadow passed over them.

They looked up. A large brown bird flew into the trees. Its wings were over ten feet long.

Ed couldn't believe his eyes. "Did you see the size of that bird?" he said.

Frank nodded. "Yes. I've never seen such a big bird."

As the sun came up over the trees, the men ate their breakfast. Frank looked down at his cup. He had not had much sleep the night before.

"I'm starting to wonder about this trip," he said.

"What do you mean?"

"I'm not sure we can make it through Silvabamba," said Frank. "I didn't think it would be like this. The Indians and all."

Ed slowly came to his feet. "It's been no picnic. And it may get worse. But what can we do? Worrying about what might happen next won't help."

Frank didn't answer.

"We can't go back, Frank. And we can't stay here. We've got to go on."

Ed picked up his pack. "Come on, Frank. Get a hold of yourself."

They set out into the jungle.

The going was slow. They moved through a jungle of trees and vines. The thick branches shut out the sun. The men stopped. Something was moving just in front of them.

Frank looked at his friend. "Indians?"

Ed shook his head. "Indians would never make that much noise."

With guns in hand, they moved slowly forward. Suddenly, a large animal came crashing out of the jungle at them. Frank and Ed both fired their guns at once.

The animal roared and crashed back into the jungle.

Frank and Ed looked at each other.

"A wild pig?" said Ed.

"I don't know," said Frank. "But whatever it was, we hit it." He pointed to blood on the ground. "Come on," he said. "Let's find it."

They followed the trail of blood. It led to a large tree. From behind the tree they could see a long, thin tail. It was the tail of the animal they had shot.

They stepped forward.

"Look out!" Ed shouted.

The animal jumped out at them. It was on Frank like a flash.

Frank brought his arm up and fell back. The animal was going for Frank's neck. But Frank grabbed the animal by its neck first. He tried to push the animal to the ground. But it twisted free and dug its teeth into Frank's arm.

"Help me!" Frank screamed.

Ed swung his gun at the animal and fired. The animal fell. It was hurt. But then it got back up and jumped at Ed. He fired again. The animal twisted on the ground. Then it lay still.

Frank and Ed looked at the dead animal. It was dark brown. It had a pointed nose and a long, thin tail. It was about three feet long.

Frank looked at the animal. "I can't believe it," he said. "It just can't be."

"It is," said Ed.

"But how could it be possible?" Frank said. "Rats are never this big."

"I don't understand it either," said Ed. "But it's a rat—a giant rat!"

CHAPTER **4**

A LAND OF GIANTS

There was blood all over Frank's arm. He reached into his pack.

"I'll do that," said Ed. He took a bandage from the pack.

Something was moving in the jungle. Ed put the bandage around Frank's arm. "More trouble?" Frank said.

"Could be," Ed answered. "Let's get out of sight."

They ran behind a log.

The jungle was very quiet. Suddenly, a giant rat came through the bushes. It was followed by other rats.

Frank and Ed ducked down behind the log. The rats went by without seeing them. Then they heard a roar.

They looked up over the top of the log. The giant rats were eating the rat Ed had killed.

"Let's get out of here," Ed whispered. One of the giant rats looked up. It spotted them. The rat started toward them. Frank and Ed started running. They could hear the rats following them. They ran as fast as they could, crashing through the thick jungle.

Frank fell. Ed helped him up. A giant rat came running at them. Ed brought up his rifle and fired.

The animal fell. Blood ran down its body. The other rats jumped on it.

Frank and Ed headed deeper into the jungle. They kept going for a long time. Finally, Frank looked back. The jungle was quiet again.

The two men stopped and fell to the ground. For a minute, they were too tired even to speak.

Then Ed pushed himself up and reached for his canteen. He drank, then handed the canteen to Frank. Still lying on the ground, Frank raised his head and drank. Ed sat with his back to a tree. Frank handed the canteen back to Ed.

"I was just thinking," Frank said. "You know, the zoos back home would really like to have some of these animals."

"Maybe we could start our own zoo," Ed said.

"If people only knew," said Frank. "Silvabamba is a lost world. I never dreamed it would be like this. Before we came here, I wondered about the things we would see. I wondered about the different people we might meet and the different animals we might see. Sometimes my thoughts would get pretty wild. I'd picture in my mind strange things we might find in Silvabamba. But never—never—did I think we would find a bird with wings over ten feet long like the one we saw this morning. Or giant rats. I can't wait to tell the world about what we have seen."

"Now I know why the Indians didn't come after us," said Ed. "I couldn't understand why they tried to get us to come back across the canyon. They must have thought that it was better for us to die at their hands than to be torn to pieces by the giant rats." Ed smiled to himself. "I guess in their own way they were trying to be kind."

"But how did these animals get here?" Frank asked. "Where did they come from?"

Ed shook his head. "That's something I'd like very much to know. But for now, I'd just like to—" Suddenly Ed screamed. Something had come up from behind him and was wrapping itself around his chest.

It looked like a snake.

Ed tried to twist free. But he couldn't move his arms.

"Help me! Help me!" he screamed.

Frank grabbed the snake and tried to pull it off his friend. Ed got one arm free. He grabbed the snake by the head. Then he saw that the snake had no eyes. It had just a small hole for a mouth.

Ed pulled at the snake's body with all his might.

Both men were fighting as hard as they could. They knocked the snake to the ground.

"Run for it," Ed shouted.

They both ran into the jungle. The snake started after them. But, because it had no eyes, it could not find them. They watched it moving around, looking for them. The snake was almost ten feet long. It had a thick, dark-red body.

At last, the snake moved off the other way.

Frank turned to his friend. "You OK?"

Ed nodded. "I've never seen a snake like that before," he said. "And I never want to see one like it again."

"Ed, that wasn't a snake," Frank said. "It was a worm."

"A *worm?!* It can't be!"

"Did you see the head?" Frank asked. "A snake doesn't have a round head like that. It was a worm, all right—a giant worm. And . . ."

Ed stopped him. "Quiet," he said. "Keep down."

Frank looked at him. "What's the matter? What is it, Ed?"

"Someone is out there."

"Where?"

"There—in the shadows."

Frank looked. At first, he couldn't see anything. Then, in the shadows, he saw two large eyes.

The eyes were looking right at them.

Suddenly, a croaking sound came from the shadows. Frank and Ed looked at each other.

There was the croaking sound again.

Something suddenly jumped out of the shadows and landed between the two men.

It was a frog—a giant frog.

The frog was three feet high. Its bottom side was white. Its body was green and yellow. The frog had a hungry look in its eyes.

They stepped back. Frank started to speak, but couldn't. His heart was pounding. Finally, he whispered, "Let's get out of here. Let's run for it."

Ed said, "Move slowly—slowly!"

The frog stopped croaking. It was getting ready to jump at Frank and Ed.

Ed put out his hand. "Stop. It's no good. Don't move, Frank. Stay still."

Frank looked at Ed. "Why?"

"If you make a fast move, the frog will jump," Ed said.

"Are you sure?"

"I watched plenty of frogs when I was a kid. They always jump when something moves."

"We can't stand here all day. We have to get out of here!"

"Don't move. Don't!"

Frank stepped back. The frog jumped. It hit Frank with its long back legs. Frank fell back. The frog suddenly opened its mouth. Its tongue flew out and twisted around Frank's leg. He felt himself being pulled toward the frog.

Ed hit at the frog with the back of his gun. The frog let go of Frank's leg.

"Look out!" Frank shouted.

Another frog jumped out of the jungle. Ed ducked. The frog's body flew over Ed's head.

Frank came to his feet. "Come on!" he shouted.

They ran. A frog jumped out in front of them. Frank brought up his gun. Before he could fire, the frog's tongue flew out and twisted around the gun. It pulled the gun out of Frank's hands.

"Never mind the gun," Ed said. "Run for it!"

Ed jumped over a log; his foot caught on a branch. He fell hard.

Frank ran back to his friend.

"My leg," said Ed. "I've twisted it."

Frank reached down to help Ed.

"No, go ahead!" said Ed. "I'll cover you."

"Nothing doing," said Frank. "We came in here together. And that is the way we're leaving—together."

"I'll only slow you down, Frank."

Frank didn't answer. He reached down and helped his friend to his feet.

From the shadows, a frog jumped at them. It hit Frank. He fell back. Lying on the ground, Ed grabbed his gun. He turned and fired. The shot missed the frog and hit a tree. Ed fired again. This time, the shot hit the frog between the eyes. The frog dropped.

Frank and Ed waited. But the jungle was quiet once more. The frogs had gone.

Frank helped Ed up. "Hold on to me," said Frank. Together, they headed up a low hill. At the top they stopped. Below them, they could see a river. Its bright, clear water was shining in the sun.

Frank looked down at the river and smiled. "I never thought a river would look so good," he said. "That's going to get us out of here, Ed. All we have to do is follow it."

"I'll be glad to leave this jungle behind—for good," Ed said. Then he looked at Frank. "And yet—just think of the great stories we can tell about Silvabamba when we get back, Frank."

Frank smiled. "Will they believe us?"

"Believe us?" said Ed. "Of course, they will. Why not?"

"Stories of giant rats? Giant worms and frogs?" Frank said. "I've seen them. Yet *I* still find them hard to believe."

"Well, I don't care if they believe me or not," said Ed. "We've been here, in Silvabamba, and we have seen things no one else has ever seen. That's enough for me."

Ed turned suddenly. "What was that?"

They listened. There was a buzzing noise in the air. It was coming from the tree Ed had fired at.

A tiny, black cloud came out of the tree. The cloud grew in size. It came over the hill. Ed and Frank looked up.

"Bees!" shouted Ed.

The bees flew down. They were as large as birds.

Frank and Ed ran down the hill. Like a dark cloud, the bees followed them.

The bees flew down over their heads. Frank and Ed hit at them with their arms.

"Come on," said Frank. They ran along the bank of the river.

Ed fell. Because of his twisted leg, he could not run fast.

"Frank," Ed called. "My leg! I can't run."

Frank ran back to Ed. The bees flew down. They buzzed all around the men.

Frank couldn't see. Bees covered his face.

"The river, Frank! The river!"

Frank ran toward the river. His body felt like it was on fire. With bees covering his face and neck, he ran into the river, pulling Ed along with him.

CHAPTER 5

SECRET OF THE PYGMIES

The river was strong. It carried them down, away from the bees.

Frank tried to swim. But the bee bites had made his body weak. He felt himself going under.

Ed swam to Frank and pulled him up. Holding Frank, Ed swam toward the river bank.

The river was wide, with many turns. Frank and Ed had seen it from the plane. From up there, the river had looked like a snake winding through the jungle.

Still holding Frank, Ed tried to reach the river bank. But the river was too strong. Water rushed over them. He tried to hold on to Frank. But he could not. He saw Frank go under.

Then Ed felt himself going under again, too. This is the end, he thought.

Slowly, Ed opened his eyes. He lay on his back in wet sand. He heard voices and turned.

Natives were standing on the river bank, a short way off. They looked like children.

Ed started to get up. The natives came down from the river bank and stood over him.

"Amigo. Friend," Ed said.

Without a word, they reached down and pulled him to his feet.

Ed looked at them. They were not children. They were pygmy men. They were only about four feet tall.

They held Ed's arms.

"Amigo. Friend," Ed said again.

The pygmies looked at each other and smiled. Their teeth were sharpened to points.

Ed looked at the river, then at the river bank. He could not see Frank. He wondered if his friend was still alive.

The pygmies pulled Ed up onto the river bank. He was too weak to fight them. His arms and face were covered with bee bites. He hurt all over.

The pygmies followed a trail that led around tall trees. Pygmy women stood near the trail, watching.

On one side of the trail, Ed saw a long hut. It was filled with cages of many different sizes. Ed tried to get a better look. But the pygmies pushed him forward.

The trail ended at a clearing. Around the clearing were small huts made of branches and leaves. Pygmy children stood in front of the huts. They looked up at Ed, wide-eyed.

One of the children held a rope. The rope was tied to an animal. It was a giant mouse—almost two feet long.

They stopped in the center of the clearing. Ed could see a circle of tall poles set in the ground. Inside the circle was a wide hole. Across the hole lay thick logs.

"Ed! Ed!" It was Frank's voice. Ed turned.

Frank stood at the end of the clearing, tied to a tree.

"Frank! You OK?" Ed called.

"Yes," said Frank. "I'm OK. These pygmies pulled me from the river. But I can't move. They have me tied to a tree."

Someone shouted. All the pygmies turned and looked at a large hut off to the right. From out of the hut stepped a pygmy woman. The other pygmies fell to their knees.

The woman was their queen, Ed decided.

The pygmy queen walked toward them. She was a short, heavy woman. Her light-brown skin was painted with yellow circles. Her rich, black hair was long and straight and had white flowers in it.

She said something to one of the pygmy men. He answered and pointed to the river.

She stepped close to Ed. She looked him right in the eyes. Her eyes seemed to be burning like fire.

Yes, she has to be their queen, Ed thought.

She reached out and touched his arm. Her touch was very light.

She looked up at him. Her dark eyes seemed to be looking right through him. Ed wondered what she was thinking.

The queen turned away. Slowly, she raised her arm and said something to the pygmies.

The pygmies grabbed Ed and pulled him toward the tree where Frank was tied. Ed tried to twist free. But it was no use. There were too many of them.

The pygmies tied Ed to the tree with Frank.

"What's going on?" Frank whispered. "What are they going to do to us?"

"It doesn't look too good," Ed answered. "They know that we know their secret."

"Secret?" said Frank. "What secret?"

"Did you see what their children use for pets?" Ed asked.

"I saw one of them with a giant mouse," Frank said. "It was as big as a dog."

"That's it," Ed said. "That's the secret. The secret of how the pygmies protect themselves."

"What do you mean?"

"The pygmies raise giant animals."

"You mean the giant rats and frogs we saw?"

"Yes," said Ed. "I think so. When the pygmies brought me here, I passed a long hut. Inside the hut were rows of animal cages. The cages were lined up in each row by size, from small to large. I saw a pygmy taking an animal from one cage and putting it in the next cage. That cage was a little larger. I don't know how they do it, Frank. But somehow they have worked out a way of raising giant animals."

Frank looked at Ed without speaking. Then he said, "I can't believe it. It's not possible."

"But it's true," Ed said. "It must be. And I also think that we have seen only some of their giant animals. I'm pretty sure there are many other kinds that we have not yet seen."

"But why, Ed? Why?"

"I think the pygmies raise the giant animals to protect themselves," Ed answered.

"Protect themselves?" Frank said. "Those giant animals could kill all the pygmies in a second. Like they almost killed us."

"I don't think so," Ed said. "Remember the Indians? Remember how they were afraid to cross the canyon after us? Now we know why."

"You think they were afraid of the giant animals," said Frank.

"Yes," Ed answered. "Remember the human teeth the Indians wore around their necks? They had to kill to get them. At one time they probably killed pygmies. The pygmies could not fight those Indians very well. The Indians are too big and strong. In time, the Indians would have killed them all. But the pygmies learned how to raise giant animals. The giant animals protect them. Now, the Indians are afraid to cross over the canyon. The pygmies are safe."

"I can see why the Indians would be afraid of the giant animals," said Frank. "But why aren't the pygmies afraid, too?"

"Why should they be?" said Ed. "You saw that pygmy boy with the giant mouse."

"Yes, I saw him."

"Well, that was the boy's pet."

Frank looked at Ed. ". . . So?"

"Did you ever have a pet?"

"Sure," Frank said. "I had a dog when I was a kid."

"Did that dog ever attack you?"

"No," said Frank.

"Did it ever attack any of your friends?"

"No. I could always control it."

"You could control your dog because you had raised it," said Ed. "And the pygmies can control their giant animals for the same reason, Frank. They have raised them as pets."

"But I still don't understand why they have us tied up," said Frank.

"Look at them," said Ed.

Standing in small groups, the pygmies were whispering and watching Frank and Ed. A little boy stood behind a tree looking at them.

"They are afraid," said Ed. We know the secret of their giant animals. And they are afraid we will tell the Indians about their secret."

For a minute, Frank didn't answer. ". . . I guess you and I are the first ones to know their secret."

He looked down at the ropes around him. "And I think they are going to make sure we are the last ones to know, too."

CHAPTER **6**

THE QUEEN DECIDES

The sun was low over the trees. Ed's body pressed against the ropes. His eyes were closed.

Frank could not sleep. He looked at the pygmies. They were throwing wood on a fire in the center of the clearing.

Sparks flew up from the fire. By the fire, pygmy women were cutting meat.

Frank remembered now that he had not had anything to eat since morning. But he was not hungry. He was too frightened.

It was dark now. The pygmies were sitting around the fire, eating. Frank looked down at the ropes around him. If only he could cut the ropes. Then he and Ed could escape into the dark jungle.

The pygmies had taken Ed's knife. Suddenly Frank thought of his watch. The pygmies had not taken that. Maybe he could use the glass from the watch to cut the ropes.

Frank twisted his hand and tapped the watch against the tree. He heard the glass break. Then he reached for a piece of the broken glass.

Holding the piece of glass with his fingers, he brought it against the rope around his arms. Slowly, he began to cut at the rope.

The glass slipped from his fingers.

He reached for another piece of glass from his watch. But the pieces that were left were too small.

It was no use. He could not cut the rope.

Maybe if he rested for a while, he would be able to think of another way to escape. There had to be a way. There just had to be.

Frank tried to force himself to think. But he could not. He felt his body pressing against the ropes. He was too tired to keep his eyes open. He felt them closing. Then he was asleep.

A dog barked. Frank opened his eyes. It was early morning.

He turned. Ed was still asleep.

The clearing was empty. The pygmies were in their huts.

Above the trees, the sky was a bright orange. For a minute, Frank did not think of where he was. He watched the beautiful jungle sun coming up over the trees.

Then a pygmy came out of a hut. Soon, other pygmies were walking around the clearing.

Frank turned to Ed. "Ed. Ed," he whispered.

Ed opened his eyes. He looked at his friend. ". . . I was dreaming," Ed said. "We were on the river, heading out of Silvabamba." He looked over at the pygmies. "There's something going on over there."

The pygmies were standing around the circle of poles in the clearing.

"What are they looking at?" Frank said.

"Something in that hole inside the circle of poles," Ed said.

The pygmies suddenly fell to their knees. The pygmy queen came out of her hut. She slowly walked over to the tree where Frank and Ed were tied. She stood looking at the two men. There was a sad look on her face. She turned and looked at the faces of her people. Then she looked again at Frank and Ed.

She was trying to decide what to do with these strange men who had come to her land.

At last, she pointed to Frank and Ed and said something.

She had decided.

The pygmies stood up. A group of pygmy men came over to her.

Now the queen turned to the other pygmies and spoke. Her voice was low. She pointed toward the river. Her black eyes flashed. Her voice became loud.

A pygmy ran forward. He picked up some dust and threw it at Frank and Ed.

The pygmy queen was speaking very fast now. The other pygmies shouted and waved their arms.

The queen was screaming at Frank and Ed now. They did not understand her words. But she sounded both angry and sad. Suddenly she raised her arms up over her head and said, *"Manatu! Manatu!"*

Frank wondered what the words might mean. He suddenly felt cold all over.

All was suddenly very quiet. Then, without a word, some of the pygmies ran forward. They started to take the ropes off Frank and Ed.

Frank looked at Ed. They knew what they had to do. If they were going to escape, they must do it now.

Frank swung at a pygmy and knocked him down. But other pygmies jumped on him. The pygmies were small, but they were strong. They pulled Frank and Ed toward the clearing. The other pygmies were all around them, shouting, *"Manatu! Manatu!"*

They pulled the men through an opening in the circle of poles. In the middle was a deep hole covered with logs. The pygmies lifted the logs that lay across the hole.

At the bottom of the hole were giant rats!

"Manatu! Manatu!" the pygmies shouted. In the hole, the rats were jumping and climbing over each other. Their sharp teeth flashed in the sun.

Standing between Frank and Ed, the queen pointed down at the rats. *"Natu manatu ani!"* she said. Frank and Ed could guess the meaning of her words. They tried to pull free from the pygmies. Ed twisted and kicked at the pygmies who held him.

The pygmies pulled him to the ground. But they had a hard time holding him.

Then Frank made a move. He threw himself back suddenly and pulled one arm free. He pushed two of the pygmies down.

Now Ed was back on his feet. He grabbed a pygmy and knocked him to the ground. Two pygmies jumped on his back. But he threw them off. Before anyone could stop him, he had grabbed the queen. He held her around the neck with one arm.

The pygmies shouted. Everyone stopped fighting at once.

The queen said something to her people. The pygmies were suddenly quiet. They were not sure what they should do.

Ed stepped back, still holding the queen. "Frank?"

"Right behind you."

"They are afraid I'll hurt their queen. They won't do anything as long as we hold her."

The queen spoke again. *"Na mati ora kani. Tuku! Tuku! Manatu ani!"*

She was telling her people not to worry about her, Ed guessed. Telling them to kill the two men. But the pygmies would not move. They did not want anything to happen to their queen.

Frank and Ed moved through the opening in the circle of poles. In the clearing, Ed turned to his friend. "Let's head for the river," he said. "We will take the queen with us."

They backed toward the trail to the river. The pygmies stood in the clearing, watching them.

They were almost to the river when the queen suddenly kicked at Ed and bit his arm. She was free!

"Get her!" Ed shouted. "If she gets away, we are dead men!"

Frank grabbed for the queen but missed. She was running back up the trail to her people.

Frank started after her. Ed called after him.

"Never mind her now! Let's get to the river. We don't have much time!"

They started running as fast as they could toward the river. The pygmies were right behind them. Their queen shouted, *"Tuku! Tuku! Manatu ani!"*

Frank and Ed ran for their lives.

CHAPTER 7
THE RIVER

The pygmies' canoes were lined up near the water. Ed pushed a canoe into the river. Frank helped him with the other canoes. They pushed all the canoes into the river, leaving just one for themselves.

Then they jumped into their canoe.

Pygmies ran along the river bank. Shouting, they splashed through the water toward the canoe.

Frank and Ed paddled the canoe out into the river as fast as they could. Pygmies started to swim after them.

Ed looked back. A hand grabbed the side of the canoe. Ed swung his paddle down hard. The hand let go.

The canoe headed down the river. A pygmy reached out and grabbed the back of the canoe.

"Look out!" Frank shouted.

Ed raised his paddle and swung it. The pygmy let go of the canoe and went under.

Ed turned to Frank. "Faster!" he shouted. "Paddle as hard as you can!"

The canoe shot through the water.

The pygmy's head popped out of the water. He looked around. The canoe was now too far away to stop. The other pygmies knew it, too. They watched as the canoe headed down the river. Their secret was lost.

Frank and Ed looked back. There was no one behind them.

They paddled the canoe around a bend in the river. The sun was shining on the water. Jungle birds called from the trees on either side of the river. That, and the splash of their paddles, was the only sound.

Frank said, "It won't be long now. We should be out of Silvabamba soon."

Ed smiled. "It can't be soon enough for me."

Frank said, "Yesterday I watched the pygmies sitting around their fire eating. I wasn't hungry then. But now I could eat a horse."

Ed laughed. "How about a rat? Are you hungry enough to eat a giant rat?"

The canoe now started to move faster through the water. The river was strong. It was pulling the canoe along.

Soon the water started to get rough. Frank and Ed had to fight to keep the canoe from turning over. They could see the rushing water break over large rocks in the river. Rough waves splashed into the canoe.

Then, as they came around another bend in the river, they heard a roaring sound. The rough water all around them seemed to be boiling.

Frank pointed and shouted. Ed could not hear him. The roaring of the river was too loud.

Suddenly, the river seemed to come to an end. A waterfall!

"Jump!" Ed shouted. "Swim for it!"

But it was too late.

The front end of the canoe shot out over the waterfall. Then the whole canoe dropped down into the crashing water.

Frank and Ed fell through the wall of roaring water.

The waterfall crashed over their heads. They were pushed under. Their bodies fell to the bottom of the river.

Many miles down the river from the water-fall, some men were fishing. They had come from the small river town of Vilamona.

They were fishing near a small island in the river. One of the men thought he saw something on the bank of the island. He paddled his canoe over to take a look.

It was Frank.

The man called to his friends. Then he jumped out of his canoe and ran over to Frank. He was still alive, but his eyes were closed. His left leg was all twisted. It was broken in two places.

The other men landed their canoes and came over. One of them pointed to another body lying near Frank. He ran over to the body and turned it over.

It was Ed. His eyes were open, but he didn't know where he was. ". . . Where? What is the . . .?" The men told him not to talk. They carried Ed to one of the canoes. "Frank . . . Where's my friend Frank?" Ed tried to move, but he was too weak. He raised his head a little and then passed out.

When the canoes reached Vilamona, a doctor was called. He had Frank and Ed taken to his house.

Ed opened his eyes. He saw the doctor working on Frank's leg.

"How is he?" Ed asked.

"He is very weak," the doctor answered.

"Will he be all right?"

The doctor nodded. "Yes. He will be all right. But he needs a lot of rest." The doctor turned to Ed. "You must rest, too."

That night, Ed lay awake. By his bed, an oil lamp gave off a weak yellow light.

Frank turned and slowly opened his eyes. He looked at Ed.

Ed smiled. "How you doing?"

Frank looked around the room. "Where are we?"

"In Vilamona—a doctor's house."

Frank put his arm on his head. ". . . I feel like I've been run over by a train."

"The doctor says you will be all right."

"What happened?" Frank asked. "How did we get here?"

"Some men who were fishing found us. They pulled us out of the river and brought us here."

"Did they ask you anything?"

"No," said Ed. "I was in no shape to talk. We can tell them the whole story about Silvabamba tomorrow . . . I guess."

They said nothing for a minute, listening to the sounds of the jungle.

Frank turned. "Ed."

"What?"

"I was thinking about the pygmies," said Frank.

"Funny. So was I," Ed said.

"What will happen to them?" Frank said.

"What do you mean?"

"What will happen when others find out their secret?"

"What will happen?" Ed said. "The same old story, I'm afraid. People from all over the world will want to see and hunt the giant animals. Catch them for zoos. And, of course, the pygmies will try to stop them—they will fight. But they can't win. Soon, the pygmies themselves will become hunted. And, in time, they will all be wiped out."

"The pygmy queen knew it, too," Frank said.

"Yes," Ed said. "The queen knew that if we got away, it would mean the end for all the pygmies. I don't think she really wanted to kill us. But she had to decide one way or the other. She only wanted to save her people."

Frank did not say anything. He was thinking.

Then he said, "We are the only ones who know so far. The waterfall keeps people from going up the river."

"Yes," Ed answered. "Because of the waterfall, no one knows about the pygmies and their secret. No one but us."

"Well, if we don't tell the pygmies' secret, no one else will ever know."

Ed looked at Frank. "What secret?"

Frank smiled.

Thinking about the lost world of Silvabamba, the men fell asleep.